CONTENTS

FORWARD

In an age where the most whimsical font can dictate the digital discourse, it takes courage to set forth on a journey unlike any other. A journey filled with pixel-perfect precision, endless imagination, and the relentless pursuit of visual excellence. Welcome to "The Designer's Odyssey: Navigating Visual Magic in a Universe Dominated by Comic Sans."

I am MSoto, your guide on this intrepid expedition through the uncharted territories of design. In these pages, you will find more than mere tutorials or lifeless lists of tools. You will discover a cosmos where creativity collides with technology, where ordinary text transforms into extraordinary art, and where Comic Sans does not reign supreme.

In my years as a designer, I have seen many fall victim to the mundane, to the ordinary, and to the safe. But why dwell in the ordinary when the extraordinary awaits? Why bow to Comic Sans when a universe of fonts, colors, and textures is at our fingertips?

Together, we will embark on a journey that explores every nook and cranny of the design universe. From the simplicity of pencil sketches to the complexity of digital interfaces, we'll uncover the principles that make designs resonate, connect, and, ultimately, enchant.

Prepare yourself, dear reader, for an odyssey of discovery and innovation. Let your creativity soar beyond the conventional, and may your designs never be confined by the earthly constraints of Comic Sans.

Happy travels,
MSoto

CHAPTER 1

BRAND ARCHITECT

In a world cluttered with business cards, logos, and flashy websites, it's the Brand Architect who holds the golden compass. Not a simple wielder of rulers and pencils, but a modern-day sorcerer who breathes life into the face of a business. And face it, if your business were a person, wouldn't you want it to look fabulous?

BUILDING THE CATHEDRALS OF COMMERCE

The Importance of Branding

First, let's lay down the foundation: What on Earth (or any other habitable planet) is branding? Is it that thing cowboys do? Well, sort of, but not exactly.

Branding is the process of creating a strong, positive perception of a company, its products, or services in the customer's mind by combining elements such as logo, design, mission statement, and a consistent theme throughout all marketing communications. It's like painting a picture of your business in the minds of your audience, except the picture is crafted with invisible ink, glitter, and a touch of magic.

When done right, a brand is more than just a snazzy logo or a catchy tagline. It's a cohesive, engaging personality that people can relate to. It's the difference between "that shoe shop around the corner" and the store where "Dreams Meet Footwear."

Graphic Designers: The Modern-Day Brand Alchemists

So, who are the magicians behind these grand cathedrals of commerce? Enter the Graphic Designer, an artist with an uncanny ability to translate wild dreams into visual realities. They're the ones who pick up the chaos of ideas, sift them through their creative colanders, and serve them on a digital platter.

A skilled Graphic Designer doesn't just create a logo. They look into the soul of the business, have a chat with it over tea, and then design something that mirrors the ethos, values, and goals of the company. They're not just drawing things, they're crafting identities.

These artists work closely with businesses, large and small, to ensure that the face of the business is not just pretty but also effective. Because what's the point of a stunning logo if it doesn't make people want to learn more about what lies behind it?

A Building Without a Blueprint is a Castle in the Sand

So, why should businesses invest in proper branding, you ask? Imagine constructing a building without a blueprint. Sounds fun, right? Until the walls start looking like abstract art and the roof decides to make friends with the floor.

A brand without a proper design is a ship without a compass. It might sail, but where? Graphic Designers are the architects of this ship. They ensure that every visual element, from the logo to the business card, resonates with the audience and sends the right message.

Conclusion

Branding isn't just about a splash of color and a fancy font. It's about creating a living, breathing personality that speaks to the audience. It's the cathedral where commerce and creativity meet, and Graphic Designers are the architects holding the keys to its gates.

So, next time you see a memorable logo or a catchy advertisement, tip your hat to the Brand Architects behind it. They're the silent heroes, painting our world one brand at a time. And who knows, perhaps they'll paint yours next!

CHAPTER 2

VISUAL STORYTELLER

Gather 'round, fellow seekers of wisdom, and let's open the second scroll of our branding odyssey. In the first chapter, we delved into the world of Brand Architects. Now, it's time to embark on a journey with the Visual Storyteller, the novelist of images, the poet of pixels, and the bard of the business world.

THE GRAPHIC NOVELIST OF THE BUSINESS WORLD

The Power of Visual Communication

Once upon a time, a picture was worth a thousand words. Today? It's worth a whole library.

In an era where the human attention span competes with that of a goldfish, visual communication reigns supreme. It's not enough to merely say something; you need to show it, and in full Technicolor splendor.

Visual communication is the art of conveying messages, ideas, and even emotions through images, colors, shapes, and typography. It's the marketing equivalent of writing a novel but using visuals instead of words.

Why is this vital? Because the human brain processes images 60,000 times faster than text. When your audience glances at a visual, they don't just see it; they feel it. They experience your brand without even reading a single word.

Graphic Designers: The Wordsmiths of Imagery

Think of Graphic Designers as the authors of visual novels. They don't use pens or typewriters (well, some might for nostalgia's sake), but tools like Adobe Photoshop, Illustrator, and their boundless creativity to paint stories without words.

A skilled Graphic Designer can take a brand's message, its very soul, and translate it into an image that resonates with the audience. They're like chefs, but instead of flavors and aromas, they mix colors, shapes, and fonts to cook up something that tickles not just the taste buds but the very soul of their audience.

Images and Typography: The Plot and Dialogue of a Visual Novel Images are the scenery, the characters, the expressions in this visual novel, while typography is the dialogue, the voice, the subtle whispers. Together, they create a narrative that doesn't need words to explain itself.

A playful font paired with a bold image might scream innovation and fun. In contrast, a sleek, minimalist design with elegant typography might convey sophistication and class. The possibilities are endless, and the only limit is imagination (and perhaps the client's budget).

Every image, every font choice is a sentence in this novel. They tell a story, portray an emotion, and create a connection between the brand and its audience. It's like watching a movie, but you're part of it. You're not just a viewer; you're an involved character.

Conclusion

Every Business Has a Story; What's Yours?

Visual storytelling isn't just a buzzword; it's an art form. It's the melody that plays in the background as your audience interacts with your brand. It's the silent ambassador of your business, speaking volumes without uttering a word.

So, what story do you want your brand to tell? Who will be its hero, and what will be its theme song? Find yourself a Graphic Designer, a visual novelist, and let them craft your tale. Because every business has a story, and yours deserves to be a bestseller.

Next time you stroll through a website or flip through a brochure, pause and appreciate the Visual Storyteller's art. They've not only created a design; they've spun a tale, a tale that you're now a part of. Welcome to the world of visual storytelling; the pages are endless, and the ink never dries.

CHAPTER 3

CREATIVE COLLABORATOR

Step right up to the third act of our grand design odyssey, where we'll dive into the bustling backstage world of the Creative Collaborator. It's time to pull back the curtain on one of the most essential aspects of graphic design – collaboration. No solo artists here, only a full-blown symphony of creativity.

THE ENSEMBLE PERFORMANCE OF DESIGN SYMPHONY

The Importance of Collaboration

In the maze of creativity, collaboration is the golden thread that leads you to the treasure trove of great work. It's like a jazz ensemble; each musician plays a part, but the magic happens when they all jam together.

In the world of graphic design, this isn't just a nice-to-have; it's a must. You see, creating a masterpiece isn't a solitary endeavor. It's a dance, a tango between the designer, the client, and other creative minds.

It's not just about what the Graphic Designer wants to create; it's about bringing the client's vision to life, integrating the expertise of other professionals, and doing it all with style and grace.

Graphic Designers: The Conductors and Composers

In this intricate symphony, the Graphic Designer acts as both conductor and composer. They're not merely following a script; they're writing it in real-time, tuning the violins, guiding the trumpets, and making sure the percussion doesn't get too carried away.

Working with clients means understanding their needs, their vision, their dreams, and sometimes, their nightmares. It's a delicate dance of empathy, creativity, and practicality. The designer must be a mind reader, a mediator, and a magician, all rolled into one.

Collaboration with other creative professionals, be it copywriters, marketers, or fellow designers, adds layers to this symphony. It's a multifaceted dialogue, a brainstorming bonanza, a melting pot of ideas, and talents.

How to Hit the High Notes Together

How can designers ensure that this collaboration hits all the high notes without descending into cacophony? Here's the secret recipe:

1. **Listening**: This isn't just about ears but understanding. Understand the client's needs, the team's insights, and the project's goals.
2. **Communicating**: Speak the language of creativity but also clarity. Clear communication keeps everyone on the same sheet music.
3. **Empathizing**: Walk a mile in your client's shoes and perhaps even wear their hat. The more you understand their world, the better you can paint it.
4. **Adapting**: Be flexible, be fluid, be like jazz. Adapt to feedback, to new ideas, and let the symphony evolve.
5. **Respecting**: Respect the expertise and opinions of everyone in the collaboration. A symphony isn't a solo; every instrument matters.

Conclusion

Creating a Masterpiece, One Collaboration at a Time

In the grand theater of graphic design, collaboration is the star performer, the encore demander, the standing ovation earner. It's where ideas meet, creativity sparks, and masterpieces are born.

So, dear reader, as you venture into the world of design, remember, you're never alone on this stage. Embrace the Creative Collaborator within you, dance with your clients, jam with your team, and let the symphony of creativity play on.

Collaboration isn't just a chapter in the playbook of design; it's the very essence of it. And in this ever-evolving concert, there's always room for more players. Pick your instrument, find your melody, and let's make some magic together.

Next stop on this odyssey? Well, you'll have to turn the page to find out. The show, after all, must go on.

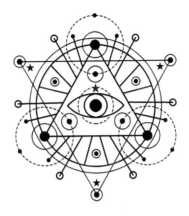

CHAPTER 4

DIGITAL DESIGNER

Fasten your digital seatbelts and hold onto your virtual hats! As we continue our design odyssey, we arrive at the bustling metropolis of modern creativity – the realm of the Digital Designer. This chapter won't just explore the neon jungle of digital design; it's a passport to the pixelated Renaissance, where graphic designers don the robes of digital alchemists.

CRAFTING VIRTUAL MASTERPIECES IN THE PIXELATED RENAISSANCE

Digital Design: A New Frontier

In the grand tapestry of creativity, digital design is a glowing thread that connects the traditional to the futuristic. It's not just about making things look good on a screen; it's about crafting interactive, immersive experiences that leap out and dance with the audience.

In the hands of a skilled Digital Designer, technology isn't a tool; it's a paintbrush, a chisel, a wand that turns the ordinary into the extraordinary. Websites become interactive journeys, apps transform into digital playgrounds, and advertisements turn into engaging stories.

Latest Trends: Surfing the Wave of Digital Innovation

The digital realm is like the ocean – vast, mysterious, and always in motion. To be a true digital explorer, you must know how to ride the waves, and oh boy, are there some exciting swells to catch:

1. **Virtual Reality (VR) & Augmented Reality (AR):** Welcome to the Matrix! Except it's fun, and you can leave anytime. These technologies are redefining interaction and immersion.
2. **3D Design & Animation:** Why stay flat when you can pop out? 3D design is giving depth, texture, and life to the digital landscape.
3. **Responsive & Adaptive Design:** One size doesn't fit all, especially in the world of screens. Designs that adapt and respond to different devices are no longer a luxury; they're a necessity.
4. **User Experience (UX) & User Interface (UI) Design:** Your audience isn't just viewing your design; they're interacting with it. Crafting intuitive, pleasurable experiences is the core of modern digital design.
5. **Dark Mode & Minimalism:** Sometimes, less is more, and darkness is light. Simplicity, elegance, and gentle-on-the-eyes themes are all the rage.

Technology: The Brush, The Canvas, The Gallery

In the hands of a Digital Designer, technology is everything and anything. Software like Adobe XD, Figma, and Blender become the art studios. Coding languages like HTML, CSS, and JavaScript turn into the palette. The Internet is the gallery, open 24/7, welcoming everyone.

It's a world where the creative process is no longer limited by physical constraints. A stroke here, a click there, a dash of code, and voila – a masterpiece born in the digital ether.

Conclusion

The Dance of Pixels, The Symphony of Bytes

Digital design isn't just a chapter in the book of creativity; it's a whole new volume. It's where art meets technology, where pixels dance, and bytes sing. It's a realm where graphic designers become explorers, innovators, and sometimes, revolutionaries.

So, dear reader, as you flip the pixels of this page, remember, you're standing at the gateway to the digital Renaissance. Whether you're a seasoned designer or a curious bystander, the virtual doors are open. Step in, explore, create, and let's craft the future, one digital masterpiece at a time.

Who knows what's next in this odyssey of design? The only way to find out is to keep on exploring. Onward, to the next pixelated adventure!

CHAPTER 5

UX/UI DESIGNER

*Prepare to embark on a thrilling
expedition as we venture into the
intricate maze of User Experience (UX)
and User Interface (UI) design. In this
chapter, we'll unravel the secrets of
creating not just pretty faces but brilliant
minds behind digital products and
services. It's not just about dazzle; it's
about direction. Welcome to the labyrinth
of user delight; the UX/UI Designer is
your guide.*

NAVIGATING THE LABYRINTH OF USER DELIGHT

UX/UI Design: A Symphony of Logic and Emotion

Imagine you walk into a dazzling palace filled with treasures, but the doors are hidden, and the hallways are a puzzle. That's a stunning interface with poor user experience. Now imagine a humble house where every door, every window invites you in, and you find treasures in every room. That's the magic of UX/UI Design.

UX/UI Design isn't just about painting pretty digital pictures; it's about orchestrating a journey, composing a symphony where logic meets emotion, where science waltzes with art.

- **User Experience (UX):** It's the compass, the map, the friendly guide that ensures users don't just visit your digital palace but enjoy every moment. It's about understanding what users want, what they feel, and what they experience as they navigate through a product or service.

- **User Interface (UI):** If UX is the map, then UI is the landscape. It's the color of the doors, the shape of the windows, the melody that plays in the background. UI complements UX by ensuring that the journey isn't just smooth but also aesthetically pleasing.

Crafting a User's Joyride: The UX/UI Designer's Toolbox

How does one become the Gandalf of digital navigation?

Here's the toolkit:

1. **Empathy Mapping:** Understanding the user's emotions, needs, and expectations is the foundation. You're not just designing for users; you're designing as them.
2. **Wireframing & Prototyping:** Sketching the skeleton, crafting the flesh, and then breathing life into the design. This iterative process helps in visualizing and refining the user's journey.
3. **User Testing:** What good is a maze if no one can walk through it? Regular user testing ensures that the design is not just beautiful but functional and user-friendly.
4. **Visual Storytelling:** Your UI must not just guide but also engage. Colors, typography, images – all these elements must tell a story, resonate with the brand, and delight the eye.
5. **Adaptation & Accessibility:** The digital world is diverse, and so are its inhabitants. Designing for different devices, different abilities, ensuring that everyone enjoys the ride – that's the hallmark of great UX/UI design.

Conclusion

The Art of Guiding, The Science of Delighting

UX/UI Design is a dance at the intersection of psychology, technology, creativity, and human intuition. It's where designers become psychologists, artists, engineers, and sometimes even wizards.

As you explore this intricate world, remember, the labyrinth of user delight isn't just a maze; it's an adventure. Every twist, every turn is a chance to surprise, to engage, to connect. It's not just about reaching the treasure; it's about enjoying the quest.

So grab your digital compass, put on your designer's hat, and let's navigate this exciting terrain. Whether you're a seasoned designer or just a curious wanderer, the world of UX/UI design awaits. Who knows what treasures you'll find, what joys you'll craft?

Next up on this design odyssey? Well, that's a secret path we'll explore together. Keep turning the pages, and let's continue this journey into the heart of creativity. The labyrinth beckons; let's unravel its mysteries, one delightful turn at a time.

CHAPTER 6

ILLUSTRATION NINJA

Prepare to step into the shadowy dojo of visual creativity, where pens and brushes replace swords and shurikens. Welcome to the realm of the Illustration Ninja, where graphic designers embrace the stealth, skill, and elegance of illustrative arts. In this chapter, we'll explore how the fine craft of illustration can add depth, personality, and a whisper of magic to your designs. Ready your artful katana; the dojo doors are open.

UNSHEATHING THE SWORD OF ARTISTIC MASTERY

Illustration: The Soulful Ink of Design

In the bustling cityscape of graphic design, illustrations are the secret alleys, the hidden gardens, the mysterious whispers. They're more than mere images; they're stories, emotions, philosophies, all penned with grace and style.

Illustration is a dance with lines and colors, where the designer, now an Illustration Ninja, moves with agility, precision, and intent. It's about adding layers, textures, soul to your work, making it not just seen but felt.

World's Best Illustrators: Senseis of the Art

The dojo of illustration is filled with legends, masters who have carved their names with ink and color.

Their work isn't just visual; it's visceral. Here are some renowned
senseis whose works we'll explore:

1. **Mary Blair:** Known for her vibrant color palettes and bold
   geometric shapes, Blair's work with Disney shaped the visuals of
   iconic movies like "Cinderella" and "Alice in Wonderland."
2. **Yoshitaka Amano:** A master of blending traditional Japanese art
   with fantasy elements, Amano's work in the "Final Fantasy" series
   has become synonymous with artistic elegance.
3. **Shaun Tan:** A storyteller with images, Tan's work in books like "The
   Arrival" illustrates the human condition without a single word,
   proving that illustrations can be powerful narratives.

These are but a few of the masters. Their work is not just to be
observed but studied, analyzed, internalized.

The Ninja's Toolkit: Techniques and Insights

How can you, too, become an Illustration Ninja? Here's your
training manual:

1. **Understanding the Story:** What's the tale behind the lines? Know it,
   feel it, live it. Every stroke should whisper a part of that story.
2. **Embracing Style:** Find your stance, your grip on the brush. Is it bold
   and abstract? Gentle and realistic? Your style is your signature.
3. **Playing with Colors and Shapes:** Color is emotion; shape is
   personality. Play with them, experiment, find the harmony that
   resonates with your message.
4. **Adding Depth and Texture:** Illustrations aren't flat; they're
   landscapes with hills and valleys. Use shadows, highlights, textures to
   give them life.
5. **Connecting with the Audience:** Your art isn't a monologue; it's a
   dialogue. What do you want your audience to feel? Guide them
   through your illustrative journey.

Conclusion

The Way of the Illustration Ninja

The path of the Illustration Ninja is one of continuous exploration, learning, and self-discovery. It's about seeing the world not just with your eyes but with your heart, your soul, your brush.

As you close this chapter, remember, the dojo never really closes. The lessons continue, the practice goes on, the ink never really dries. Whether you're a seasoned illustrator or a curious novice, the way of the Illustration Ninja is open to all.

So unsheath your artistic sword, bow to the masters, and let's continue this exciting journey through the hidden gardens of creativity. What's next in this design odyssey? Ah, that's a path we'll explore together. Keep your senses alert, your mind open, and let's move forward, one artful step at a time. The way of the Illustration Ninja awaits.

CHAPTER 7

TYPOGRAPHY WIZARD

In the enchanting world of design, typography is the ancient spellbook, the mystical runes, the sacred incantations that breathe life into the page. Welcome to the secretive guild of the Typography Wizard, where graphic designers become sorcerers, wielding the power of type to create beauty, meaning, and magic. Open the tome, light the candles, and let's delve into the alchemy of letters and words.

CONJURING THE MAGIC OF LETTERS AND WORDS

Typography: The Invisible Art that's Everywhere

Typography is like the wind – you don't see it, but you feel its presence everywhere. It's the choice of typeface, the spacing between letters, the rhythm of lines that turns ordinary text into a visual symphony. It's not just about readability; it's about personality, voice, emotion. It's the quill with which the soul of a design is penned.

In the hands of a Typography Wizard, type becomes more than mere characters; it becomes architecture, music, poetry.

The Spellbook: Anatomy of Typography

To become a true wizard of type, one must understand the anatomy of typography, the bones, the flesh, the essence.

Here are the essential elements:

1. **Typefaces & Fonts:** Serif or Sans Serif? Display or Script? Each typeface has a personality, a voice, a mood. Fonts are the different weights and styles within a typeface.
2. **Line Length & Spacing:** How long should a line be? How much space between lines? It's about rhythm, harmony, creating a reading experience that's not just comfortable but delightful.
3. **Hierarchy & Contrast:** What's more important? What needs to stand out? Using size, weight, color to create hierarchy, emphasis, and balance.
4. **Alignment & Grids:** Left, right, centered? The alignment and grid structure bring order, coherence, and sometimes a touch of chaos when needed.
5. **Legibility & Readability:** Can you read it? More importantly, do you want to read it? Designing for clarity, engagement, connection.

Masters of the Craft: Inspirational Typography Wizards

The guild of Typography Wizards is rich with legends, masters who've penned magic with type. From Jan Tschichold's modernist elegance to Paula Scher's typographic landscapes, their work is a study in beauty, innovation, and wisdom.

Conjure Your Own Magic: Practical Spells and Techniques

Ready to don your wizard's robe and wield your typographic wand?

Here's how you start:

1. **Know Your Audience:** Are you penning a love letter or casting a battle cry? Understand who you're speaking to.
2. **Choose Wisely:** Select typefaces that resonate with the message, the brand, the feeling you want to invoke.
3. **Experiment with Harmony and Contrast:** Play with sizes, weights, colors. Find the balance that sings.
4. **Mind the Details:** Kerning, tracking, leading – the tiny adjustments that turn good into great.
5. **Craft with Love and Respect:** Type is art. Treat it with the love, respect, and curiosity it deserves.

Conclusion: The Neverending Journey of the Typography Wizard

The path of the Typography Wizard is not a destination; it's a journey. It's about continuous learning, observation, experimentation. It's about seeing the world not just in pictures but in letters, words, stories.

As you close this mystical chapter, remember, the quill never really leaves your hand; the spellbook is never really shut. Whether you're a seasoned wizard or a curious apprentice, the guild of typography is open, welcoming.

What awaits in the next chapter of this design saga? Ah, that's a secret that only the pages ahead can reveal. So keep your wand ready, your eyes wide, and let's continue this magical odyssey through the realms of creativity. The world of Typography Wizards awaits, filled with beauty, wisdom, and endless enchantment. Let's conjure the magic together, one letter at a time.

CHAPTER 8

BRANDING GURU

In the pantheon of design, the Branding Guru sits atop, weaving together the threads of aesthetics, strategy, communication, and technology. In this mystical chapter, a unique ally joins your quest: ChatGPT, the digital oracle. Together, we will forge a comprehensive guide to using this formidable tool to aid your journey through each chapter, offering helpful prompts, insights, and a sprinkle of artificial wisdom. Ready to summon the oracle? Let's chant the incantations.

SUMMONING CHATGPT, YOUR DIGITAL ORACLE

The Branding Guru: A Symbiosis of Art and Science

Branding is not merely a logo or a slogan; it's a living, breathing entity, a philosophy, a soul that encapsulates an organization's essence. It's the harmonious blend of visuals, narratives, emotions, and values.

And now, with the aid of technology, like ChatGPT, this harmony can be fine-tuned, enriched, and made to sing across platforms, audiences, and cultures.

ChatGPT: Your Digital Familiar

ChatGPT is more than a tool; it's an ally, a familiar that accompanies you through the winding paths of design. It's powered by artificial intelligence but guided by human intuition, creativity, and ethics.

Here's how ChatGPT can be your guide, your mentor, your collaborator:

1. **Ideation Helper:** Stuck with a concept? ChatGPT can brainstorm with you, offering suggestions, insights, even a touch of unexpected genius.
2. **Content Crafting:** Need to pen the perfect slogan, the soulful story? ChatGPT can help you write, edit, refine.
3. **Design Critique:** Looking for an unbiased eye? ChatGPT can review your work, provide feedback, even challenge your thinking.
4. **Research Assistant:** Need insights, statistics, trends? ChatGPT can scour the digital world, gather information, even analyze patterns.
5. **Ethical Compass:** ChatGPT can help you navigate the complex landscape of ethics in design, ensuring that your work resonates with integrity and empathy.

Helpful Prompts: The Branding Guru's Spellbook

Here's a selection of magical prompts that you can ask ChatGPT, tailored for each chapter's theme:

1. **For the Graphic Designer:** "ChatGPT, can you show me examples of minimalist logo designs?"
2. **For the Visual Storyteller:** "ChatGPT, what are the latest trends in visual storytelling in advertising?"
3. **For the Creative Collaborator:** "ChatGPT, how can I improve collaboration between designers and developers?"
4. **For the Digital Designer:** "ChatGPT, what tools should I use for responsive web design?"
5. **For the UX/UI Designer:** "ChatGPT, can you help me create a user persona for a fitness app?"
6. **For the Illustration Ninja:** "ChatGPT, what's the history of caricature art?"
7. **For the Typography Wizard:** "ChatGPT, how can I pair serif and sans-serif fonts effectively?"

Conclusion: The Branding Guru and the Digital Oracle

The path of the Branding Guru is filled with wonders, challenges, wisdom, and now, with the companionship of a digital oracle, ChatGPT. It's about embracing technology not as a replacement but as an enhancement, a catalyst, a muse.

As you move forward in your design odyssey, remember, ChatGPT is there, waiting to help, challenge, inspire. It's a tool shaped by human brilliance and powered by artificial intelligence.

What awaits beyond this chapter? Ah, the adventure never truly ends; it merely transforms, evolves, beckons with new horizons. So keep your creative fires burning, your digital quill inked, and let's continue this wondrous journey through the landscapes of creativity. The world of the Branding Guru awaits, filled with knowledge, artistry, and endless potential. With ChatGPT by your side, who knows what magic you'll conjure, what heights you'll reach?

The path beckons. Let's walk it together, one inspired step at a time.

CHAPTER 9

MARKETING MAVEN

In the grand finale of our design odyssey, we arrive at the bustling bazaar of commerce, where creativity meets strategy, aesthetics embraces metrics, and the Marketing Maven reigns supreme. Here, the tools, skills, and insights gleaned from the previous chapters converge, forming a powerful arsenal that graphic designers wield to help businesses create engaging, persuasive, unforgettable marketing materials. Gather your newfound knowledge; the market awaits, vibrant, chaotic, brimming with potential.

WEAVING THE TAPESTRY OF DESIGN MASTERY INTO BUSINESS TRIUMPH

The Marketing Maven: Orchestrator of Success

Marketing is not merely selling; it's storytelling, connecting, inspiring. It's about understanding needs, desires, fears, and dreams and weaving them into a tapestry that resonates, compels, endures.

The Marketing Maven is an alchemist, a strategist, a poet, and a visionary. Utilizing graphic design as both an art and a science, the Maven crafts messages that don't just reach audiences but touch their hearts, spark their minds, move their souls.

Newfound Tools: The Maven's Treasure Chest

Through the chapters of this book, you've gathered tools, techniques, wisdom:

- **Graphic Design:** The foundation, where form meets function.
- **Visual Storytelling:** The narrative, where images speak louder than words.
- **Collaboration:** The teamwork, where ideas become innovations.
- **Digital Design:** The technology, where pixels become experiences.
- **UX/UI Design:** The empathy, where design thinks, feels, cares.
- **Illustration:** The artistry, where ink becomes emotion.
- **Typography:** The eloquence, where letters dance, sing, persuade.
- **Branding:** The essence, where businesses become brands.
- **ChatGPT:** The ally, where AI becomes a partner in creativity.

These are your treasures, your armory, the ingredients of your marketing magic.

Weaving the Magic: Graphic Designers in the Marketing Arena

How do you, the graphic designer, become the Marketing Maven?

How do you wield your newfound tools to craft marketing materials that not only sell but inspire, empower, delight? Here's the path:

1. **Understanding the Audience:** Know their hearts, their minds, their pulse. What do they need, what do they seek, what moves them?
2. **Crafting the Message:** It's not what you say; it's how you say it. Find the words, the images, the rhythm that resonates.
3. **Designing with Purpose:** Every color, every line, every font must serve a purpose, tell a part of the story, add a layer to the experience.
4. **Measuring Success:** Marketing is both art and science. Track, analyze, learn from the numbers, but never lose the human touch.
5. **Embracing Ethics:** Be honest, be respectful, be compassionate in your marketing. Let your work be a beacon of integrity.
6. **Adapting and Innovating:** The market changes; so must you. Keep learning, growing, exploring new horizons.

Conclusion: The Journey's End and a New Beginning

As we close this book, the market's noise fades, but its energy lingers, its lessons endure, its challenges beckon. You, the graphic designer, now stand as a Marketing Maven, armed with tools, enriched with knowledge, inspired with possibilities.

The journey through these chapters was a path of discovery, creativity, mastery. But it's not the end; it's a threshold, a new beginning. The market awaits, vibrant, diverse, teeming with opportunities to create, to connect, to make a difference.

With this newfound wisdom, what will you create? What stories will you tell? What lives will you touch? The answers are yours to pen, the path yours to walk, the magic yours to weave.

Go forth, Marketing Maven, and let your creativity soar, your strategies triumph, your integrity shine. The world of marketing awaits, not just as a business but as an art, a science, a human connection. May your work not just sell but inspire, not just persuade but empower, not just reach but resonate.

THANK YOU

*Thank you for this journey, this
adventure, this odyssey through the
landscapes of creativity. May it be a
source of inspiration, a catalyst for
innovation, a beacon for your path ahead.
Until our paths cross again, dear reader,
create with passion, design with purpose,
market with heart. The tapestry is yours
to weave, the magic yours to conjure, the
success yours to embrace.
Farewell, and may your designs always
shine.*

www.ingramcontent.com/pod-product-compliance
Lightning Source LLC
Chambersburg PA
CBHW061057050326
40690CB00012B/2656